Self Storage Domination

The Actions You Must Take To Dominate Your Competition

Jim Ross

ISBN: 1539125173
ISBN 13: 9781539125174
Library of Congress Control Number: 2016918846

More Praise for Self Storage Domination

"Self Storage Domination reflects Jim Ross' experience in the industry. His pragmatic approach creates an easy read for us; a great hands-on, get-it-done guide. Jim lists the many tasks required to succeed in self storage - an industry whose complexity outsiders still manage to underestimate - and organizes them in clear, actionable steps."

Markus Hecker, SiteLink

"Wow! My head is spinning right now with thoughts and plans of how I can make my self storage business even better. Reading this book was like getting a college degree in self storage management. The amount of information is extensive, but then the bonus of "resources available", beyond the pages of this book, are exhaustive. This book belongs in the bookshelf of every self storage facility, where it can be studied daily for domination of the facility's market!"

Gary Fawson, Owner

"SpareFoot has been working with storage companies since 2008 to market their facilities to new tenants. Anything that supports standing out from the competition, like the recommendations made in Jim Ross' book, will help them thrive."

Chuck Gordon, Co-Founder and CEO of SpareFoot.com

"I found Self Storage Domination to be an insightful, detailed look into how, with simple tools and resources, you can kick up your self storage game. Jim's call to action tips and extra resources are going to come in handy at all my locations. I would highly recommend Self Storage Domination to anyone who is looking to be the BEST in their current self storage market."

Shelby Beck, Vice President NSSA / Extra Self Storage-President Of Business Operations

"Self Storage Domination is a terrific resource for those starting in the self-storage industry and those who need a refresher course to pump up their operations. Jim's real world experience shines through in every chapter."

Jeff Greenberger, Selfstoragelegal.com

"Set aside all your operations and marketing books; Jim nails it for us independent storage owners! His generous and in depth book is a how to book complete with resources and action plans...it has become the centerpiece of my business operations!"

Helen C. Helton, Owner

"Jim shares valuable tools and steps that he has learned from his own hands-on experience managing facilities that will help readers to find success while they grow their self-storage businesses."

Randy Tipton, Universal Insurance

"If only I could have had this when I started in the storage industry 11 years ago, what a great help it would had been. Folks this is not just a book to read when getting started in the storage industry but a tool to refer to and review on an annual basis. You want to know success in the storage industry? Read this book."

Dean Sparks, Owner

"I appreciate that we have people like Jim Ross in our industry willing to take the time to write a book that will definitely be around as a tool to help both new or seasoned veterans in the self storage industry."

Damon Emerson, Partner- Storsmart Insurance

INTRODUCTION

Introduction

I have something to say about building, running, and growing a self storage business. This book isn't based on theories. It's based on experience. I've been in the storage industry for twenty years. I started as a storage manager while I put myself through college. I've been a regional manager for multiple properties for many more years. I ran a storage auction company for years. I've been involved in some ownership along the way as well. All my years of experience have culminated in creating my company, 3 Mile Domination.

Many self storage properties are not run at their highest efficiencies, and many times there is room for a dramatic improvement, which is why I wrote this book.

My goal is to give you everything you need to market, get rentals, and dominate your storage market. I love helping clients bring in those extra rentals and maximize their profitability for their business.

You have found this book for a reason. It's time to take the action steps necessary to dominate in this increasingly competitive marketplace. And it is becoming more competitive each and every day. The big boys of the industry are growing bigger and stronger by the minute. Make no mistake: they want to put you out of business yesterday, and they are doing everything they can to do exactly that! If you're lucky enough to be in a market where you don't have much competition, especially from the big boys, get ready, because they're coming!

In order to remain competitive, you need to have the mentality of this is mine: this is my business. I'm not going to be pushed around anymore. Draw a ring around your facility (3 Mile Domination—get it?), and say this target market is mine.

First, we'll start by preparing your self storage business for success. As they say, preparation is the key to success. We'll take your business down to the basic building blocks. We'll be giving you action items to complete that will be necessary to have a foundation to build upon. Then we'll build upon that foundation. You'll be given action steps to complete that will bring you leads, increase your rentals, grow your revenue, and dominate your self storage market. Now, let's get on with it.

ACTION,

RESOURCES,

VALUE

ACTION, RESOURCES, VALUE

Throughout this book you will see the following:

Action

Don't waste your time by just reading through this book. This book is designed for you to take action and build a dominating self storage business. When you see this icon, take the necessary action!

Resources

There are many free tools, downloads, and other resource links that compliment this book. Simply go to 3miledominators.com to create a username and password to have access to these useful items.

Value

This is the section that demonstrates results when action is taken and the impact it can have on the value of your self storage business.

In order to fully understand where the numbers are coming from in this section, you must understand a few things first. There are only two factors that affect property value: net operating income (NOI) and the capitalization rate (cap rate).

What is *NOI*? It is simply the money left after all operating expenses are paid, excluding debt service and depreciation. For example, if your annual revenue is $500,000 and your annual costs are $165,000, your NOI is $335,000. Generally the expenses of your storage property will remain pretty consistent, so it's important to focus on what you can control—generating income. The income of the storage business is ultimately what drives the value.

Throughout this book I will be using 3MD Storage as our hypothetical facility going through this action plan and how taking action is increasing the value of its facility. I will use a cap rate of 8 percent to illustrate the examples.

What is a *cap rate*? You've probably heard people talking about cap rates going up or down, or you may have heard someone say "I just sold my facility on a six cap" or "Cap rates are low in my state." What does it mean? Basically, when people talk about cap rates, they are talking about the value of their self storage facility. The way the math works is, the lower the cap rate, the higher the value of the facility. So when someone says that the cap rates are down, he or she means that an investor will pay a higher price (value) for his or her storage business.

There are many characteristics that will have an effect on the cap-rate value assigned for a self storage business, such as size, historical occupancy, competition, visibility, demographics, construction type, and so on.

Example

If you take the additional revenue a specific action brings in to your facility and divide it by the market cap rate, which is what an appraiser will do when appraising your facility, you get the value to the business that additional income creates.

So for example: 3MD Storage implemented a strategy that raised its merchandise sales an average of $300 more a month, which equals to $3,600 a year. Let's be very conservative and use an 8 percent cap rate. That additional $3,600 a year adds a value of $45,000 extra to its self storage business. ($3,600 ÷ 0.08 = $45,000).

3MD Storage

Throughout this book I will be illustrating examples using 3MD Storage. This hypothetical self storage facility has the following characteristics:

- It has 500 non-temperature-controlled units.
- The average customer rate is $100.

  Gross Potential ÷ Total Units = Average Customer Rate
  Its monthly Gross Potential is $50,000, and it has 500 units.

  $50,000 ÷ 500 = $100

- Its ALV (Average Lifetime Value) is $1,200

  Average Customer Rate × Average Length of Stay = Average Lifetime Value
  Its Average Customer Rate is $100, and its Average Length of Stay is 12 months.

  $100 × 12 = $1,200

  (We will discuss how to calculate your Average Length of Stay in the Average Lifetime Value section.)

- Expenses are 33 percent of income.

  (It averages $42,000 a month in income and has $14,000 a month in expenses.)

- The cap rate for valuation is 8 percent.

Section One:
Preparation

THE DISTANCE BETWEEN YOUR DREAMS AND REALITY IS CALLED

ACTION

DREAMS   REALITY

Domination Mind-Set

Your identity—the way you define your self storage business—will have a profound effect on taking action toward improving your facility and ultimately dominating your market.

Believe in yourself and your facility.
Start by firmly believing that your facility is already the best facility in your market and the obvious choice for customers to store their items with.

Set measurable goals.
Have measurable goals that will bring you closer every day to domination. What are your physical and economic occupancy goals? By what date do you want to meet those goals?

Accept the challenge.
Accepting challenges is an essential piece in having a successful self storage business, and it is what will create the growth of your business. For this reason bless each challenge. Take on each challenge, and take action as necessary. Each challenge is directing you toward the storage business you've always wanted.

Create Love and Purpose.
This is specifically speaking to the managers that will make or break the success of your self storage business. Be willing to love and find purpose in all aspects of what your job requires; commit to your job, and see what you're doing for the benefit of others. When you love the business you're in, there is nothing that can keep you from wanting to work at it, nurture it, and make it grow. It's time to dominate. Let's get started.

Make a decision today that you are going to dominate your local self storage market.
Spend fifteen minutes articulating your thoughts on paper about (1) how your business is going to be the elite storage facility in your market and (2) why it's important to you.

3miledominators.com
Item: You Bring About What You Think About

4

10%
OF ALL
HOUSEHOLDS
USE
STORAGE

Your Target Market

According to the 2016 edition of the Self-Storage Almanac, on average 10 percent of all households use storage. That's an amazing figure that has stayed steady for years! I love to put a figure to who my target market is and what it will take to occupy a facility.

For example, if you run a five-hundred-unit facility and there are thirty-five thousand households within a three-mile radius of your facility, to fully occupy you only need 1.5 percent (500 divided by 35,000 = 1.5%) of that local market to become customers. Self storage is a very locally targeted market. Your customers are close, you are conveniently located, and you can inexpensively deliver them a message that motivates them to use you rather than your competition.

All of your marketing tactics should focus on those who live or work by your facility. Period! I'm sure you will be shocked at how many people are in your target market, and you will see that you only need a small percentage of those who are already in the market to use storage to store with you.

Quantify what percentage of the people in your target market it will take to fill up your facility.
I love this company! Go to www.stortrack.com and click on InSite Reports.
Put your address in, and set your radius to three miles. In a few seconds you will see the population numbers around you and some other great info. From there, simply divide your total number of units by the total population in your target market to get the percentage of people in your target market needed to fill up your facility.

This part of the service from stortrack.com is currently free; however, I strongly recommend supporting them and paying the one-time fee for the full in-depth InSite Report.

3miledominators.com

Item: Resource Links

AVERAGE LIFETIME CUSTOMER VALUE OF JUST ONE EXTRA RENTAL!

5x5: $1197
5x10: $1659
10x10: $2625
10x15: $3402
10x20: $4116

Average Lifetime Value

Do you know the average lifetime value of your customer? In other words, do you know how much income an average rental brings into your self storage business? If you don't, you're not alone. Most people don't. A down-and-dirty example would be as follows:

The average unit price at your facility is one hundred dollars.

The average customer at your facility stays twelve months.

The average lifetime value for your facility is $1,200 ($100 x 12).

Now, I have seen these numbers change dramatically based on the actual average unit price and length of stay. I've seen some sites where the average length of stay is over four years!

It's important to know what the number is. As we move through this book, we will be reflecting on this number time and time again. In a nutshell, once you know what the number is, every time that phone rings or that customer walks through your doors, that's how much money is potentially on the line to come into your self storage business. When you know that number, the sales call will be more focused. When you know that number, those auction schedules will be timely. When you know that number, your marketing efforts will be a much easier decision to make— you can calculate how many rentals you will need to recoup your marketing investment. It all starts with knowing your average lifetime customer value.

So let's break it down on how I like to calculate this number. You should be able to find all the required information in the reports from your storage software.

Step 1: Pull a rent roll. You should be able to export this into Excel. From there, sort from the fewest days occupied to the most days occupied.

Step 2: Delete the first 10 percent of those units listed from the least days occupied, and then delete the bottom 10 percent of those units that have been there the longest. So for example, if you have five hundred units rented, delete the first fifty units and then scroll down and delete the final fifty units listed. That way you will have a good representation of your facility—those who have just barely moved in and those who are the lifers will otherwise skew your results.

Step 3: Average Customer Rate: Total up the columns with the rate of the units and divide by the number of units that are in this sample. This will give your average rental rate of current rented units.

Step 4: Average Length of Stay: Total up the total days occupied and divide by the number of units that are in this sample.

Step 5: Average Customer Rate x Average Length of Stay = Average Lifetime Value

Example: $135 x 11.3 = $1,525.50

Now, if your storage business has been up and running for under one year, I recommend simply using your Average Rental Rate x 12 months.

Go through Steps 1–5 today, and calculate your average lifetime value.

Write this number down somewhere where the manager who is doing sales calls can see it while conducting a phone sales presentation.

3miledominators.com
Items: Video Tutorial, Every Call Counts

What Is Measured Improves

If I asked you how many rentals you received last month from drive-by, could you give me an answer? What if I ask you what your current lead conversion percentage is? There is no reason not to have the answer to these questions at your fingertips. Many storage management software will have this simple tracking built in. However, a good ol' simple spreadsheet will do wonders as well.

An interesting thing will start happening the moment you start tracking all of your calls and rentals and how they found you—your conversions will start to increase. I've seen it time and time again. What gets measured improves.

It takes money to make that phone ring and to have a customer walk through your door. You must be tracking where your leads are coming from. Tracking is crucial to any marketing you are doing for your storage facility. By simply tracking where your leads and rentals are coming from, you can create more cost-effective marketing efforts that will get you the result you want without wasting money.

The bottom line is, if you are not tracking, you are not marketing.

Go to resources and download a template of our ROI Console (Return On Investment Console) to begin tracking immediately. Your storage software may also be able to help you track this information.

3miledominators.com
Item: ROI Console

3MD Storage began tracking every single phone call and walk-in three months ago. During that time, it noticed that its conversion percentage (leads that came in versus rentals) increased from 65 percent in the first month to 73 percent by the end of the third month of tracking. By simply having its eyes on its numbers, it was renting an extra five units a month on the same amount of leads coming in, without spending an extra dollar on advertising.

- **Additional Revenue Created: $6,000**

  5 additional rentals a month at $1,200 Average Lifetime Value

  (5 × $1,200 = $6,000)

- **Additional Value Created: $75,000**

  $6,000 additional revenue on an 8 Cap

  ($6,000 ÷ 0.08 = $75,000)

COMPETITION IS A SIGN THAT YOUR MARKET HAS GREAT POTENTIAL.

Competition Is A Sign That Your Market Has Great Potential

Competition. We all have it. And just in case you are one of the very few who currently do not have any competition, well, get ready—because it's coming before you know it. You want to have some systems in place to keep tabs on what is going on in your market. The first step in this competition section is—drum roll, please—list all your competitors!

Generally a three-mile ring around your facility is more than adequate to get a great idea of your market.

The cheapest way to find your competition is to do a simple Google search. Just type "self storage by" and your address. This will provide you a list of sites right by you. Now if you want to take this to the next level, use the service at stortrack.com that I mentioned earlier. On this site you put in your facility address and then say how big of a mile ring you want around your facility. Click a button, and the next thing you know you're staring at all of your competition. Play around on the site. They do a lot of the work regarding your competition and their online prices. Now, it's not free, but you can do a trial to see if it works for you.

Put all of your competition into a spreadsheet: name, address, phone number, website, pricing, and so on. Download the spreadsheet to fill in from our resources page, and check out stortrack.com.

3miledominators.com
Items: Competition Spreadsheet, Resource Links

COMPETITION IS A GOOD THING - IT FORCES US TO DO OUR BEST

Competition Is A Good Thing—It Forces Us To Do Our Best

OK. So you have the list of all your competition. What do you know about them? Have you ever actually driven by the site or, better yet, shopped them?

I'm a firm believer in knowing your competition inside and out, know exactly what you're up against in your market. Maybe you are in a highly competitive market, and after doing five minutes of research about your competitors, reality hits you that it's time to step up your game if you are going to compete and run a successful self storage business.

Put yourself in your customer's shoes. Most of the time, the customer's first contact with a your business is by phone. So it should be obvious that you should secret shop your competition (acting like a customer) so you can see exactly how good your competition is at sales calls. Right away, you will be able to tell on the phone who the winners and the stinkers are in your area. The point is, you are gathering intelligence on how you can position yourself as the obvious choice for a customer to rent from.

Call every one of your competition, and act like a customer inquiring about renting a storage unit. Fill out an evaluation form for each one.

3miledominators.com
Item: Sales Call Evaluation

17

REMEMBER YOUR COMPETITOR IS ONLY A MOUSE CLICK AWAY.

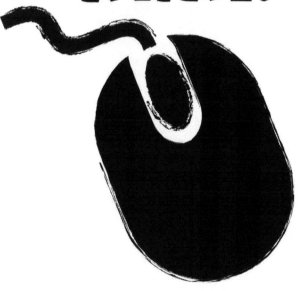

Remember, Your Competitor Is Only A Mouse Click Away

If you're not willing to update your website to a fantastic converting website along with an effective local SEO (search engine optimization) strategy, you may as well pack it up and call it game over. In this competitive market, you must have an amazing website and local SEO strategy—period!

Having a local SEO program takes time, energy, and understanding of Internet marketing. Luckily for you there will be a link to download a resource that goes into detail for you. For the purposes of this book, I simply want to point out that without a local SEO program, it's unlikely you will appear on, or even near, the first page of the search results; and if your competitors are working their local SEO, they are more likely to get those new customers instead of you.

Over 50 percent of all searches are from mobile devices. If your website isn't mobile friendly, you're sunk. Your potential customers will simply click on your competitor's mobile-responsive site and forget all about you.

If you own and operate a self storage business without a local SEO plan and mobile-responsive website, don't expect to be showing up on the first page of Google. Without taking action, your business will be lost in the shuffle. With everyone searching before they call and rent, your lack of visibility will eventually lead to new rentals drying up.

This is reality, and it's happening to storage businesses right now. You must optimize for local search to stay in the game. Simple as that.

Enter your website domain at https://www.google.com/webmasters/tools/mobile-friendly to see if your website is currently mobile friendly.

Call some website builders to evaluate and grade your website. They will do this for free. They obviously want your business, but you will have a report giving you the guidelines on what needs to be done to improve your website. Go to the website, Grader.com, to grade your website.

3miledominators.com
Items: Website Evaluation Spreadsheet, Self Storage SEO E-book, Elements Of A Good Website

IT'S GOOGLES WORLD AND WE'RE JUST LIVING IN IT.

It's Google's World, And We're Just Living In It

Again, the topic of Internet marketing for your self storage business can be a book by itself. Most owners will have a reputable service manage that portion of their marketing anyways; however, some are more hands on. This section will give you the control over an important piece to local online marketing.

It's vitally important to claim your business listing on Google My Business. This feeds your info to Google Maps and gives you some of that precious Google juice we all need.

If you are searching on a mobile device (and we all are, which means so are your customers), you will see that you have to scroll down to see organic results. As of the time of this writing, there are now only the top three Google local results being shown. You must hit "more places" to see the rest of the local storage listings in your area. Obviously, you want to be in the top three to get the most eyeballs on your business!

Having this listing optimized is extremely important. It's the centerpiece and is fundamental to any online local search. Your business simply doesn't exist if you don't create and optimize a Google My Business page for your facility.

There are a ton of simple guides to walk you through optimizing your listing, but start off going directly to Google itself at https://www.google.com/business.

Here are some good starting points:

- First, claim your listing. It's amazing how many self storage sites I still see out there that haven't done this. Don't be one of them!
- Ensure your details are up to date.
- Double check your opening hours and phone number, as these often change over time or with new owners or management.

- Check the business images you are using, and consider refreshing them or uploading higher-resolution versions.

Take out your phone (I'm sure it's within two feet of you at all times), and search for self storage in your area to see where your business comes up. If your business is there, congrats! There is still more to do to stay there. If you're not there, optimize your listing today! Take up to ten photos of your facility. These images will be used for your website, Google My Business listing, and other places coming up shortly. Get shots from the street view, aisles, some open units, office, merchandise display, and happy customers moving in (with their permission of course—no paparazzi shots). You get the idea. Showcase your facility.

Item: Link To Steps To Claim And Optimize Your Google My Business Listing

3MD Storage claimed and optimized its Google My Business listing. Within a few months, it began to receive calls from potential customers of this listing. On average it could see it was renting an additional four units a month from this source.

- **Additional Revenue Created: $4,800**
  4 additional rentals a month at $1,200 Average
  Lifetime Customer Value
  (4 x $1,200 = $4,800)
- **Additional Value Created: $60,000**
  $4,800 additional revenue on an 8 Cap
  ($4,800 ÷ 0.08 = $60,000)

VIDEO IS KING

Video Is King

I'm a big believer in the power of video. Putting focus on incorporating video into your marketing efforts will reward you with more rentals by, once again, differentiating yourself from your competition and showcasing that you are the best facility in your market.

You only have ten seconds to grab your visitors' attention when they land on your site before they click away. So create an impact by having a video on your website. Even those slideshow videos that you see are still way better than having nothing at all.

The first few minutes a potential customer spends on your website is crucial to building trust and credibility. Plus, an added benefit of having media like this on your website is that it helps with your rankings on Google!

Here are some interesting statistics about video marketing:

- Seventy-two hours after visiting any website, people remember only 10 percent of the text, 65 percent of images and visuals, and 90 percent of videos.
- People searching on their phones (that's everyone!) are three times as likely to view a video as desktop or laptop users are.
- Videos on landing pages can increase conversions by up to 80 percent.

When you were researching your competitors' websites (you did that, right?), how many of them had videos as part of their marketing on their websites. I'm sure it's safe to assume not many, if any of them did at all. Can you see how putting together a simple video could really help you stand out when someone is looking for a storage place to rent?

Now, you may be thinking that you don't want to be on camera and that you have no idea how to shoot and edit a video. I came across this concern many, many times, which is why I created an animated video that can be customized to your facility. It's unique and memorable. If you are not camera shy (or can find someone to put in the video who isn't shy), it's not that difficult nowadays to put something together quickly. You already have a great video recording device in the palm of your hands. Use your phone to do a simple walking tour of your facility. Act as if you're talking with a potential customer who walked through your doors. Showcase your office, get on the golf cart, or walk to a unit. Roll up the door, and showcase how the unit is secured. Demonstrate the coded gate access and the security cameras. Invite the customer to call you to rent.

You don't have to be Steven Spielberg here. Some simple shots and a quick edit will put you way ahead of others in your area.

Take a look at the video at the resource link. You're welcome to model the structure to be able to quickly film and edit a video to put on your website. Make it a goal to have a video done within a week. There is no need for it to take longer. If having it edited is a sticking point for you, there are many places online that would be happy to help you edit the video footage you have into something that looks very professional. Take a look at sites like www.weedit.com, www.upwork.com, or www.animoto.com to see what they can do for you for very little money.

3miledominators.com
Item: Links To View Videos

3MD Storage created a video to put on the homepage of its website. Although it can't quantify if having the video was the deciding factor in convincing potential renters to call it instead of its competition, it was sure that it was at least getting one additional rental a month from having an element on its website that helped it stand out from its competitors.

- **Additional Revenue Created: $1,200**
  1 additional rental a month at $1,200 Average Lifetime Value
  (1 x $1,200 = $6,000)
- **Additional Value Created: $15,000**
  $1,200 additional revenue on an 8 Cap
  ($1,200 ÷ 0.08 = $15,000)

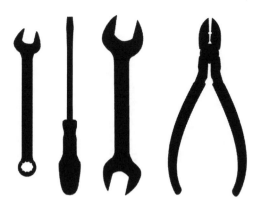

WARNING HIGH MAINTENANCE...
(NOT REALLY)

Warning: High Maintenance—Not Really

I've seen it happen to too many self storage sites: at one time they were brand new, the managers took pride in their facility, and the owners were excited about their new investment. Then the years wore on, everyone became complacent, and the everyday maintenance issues and focus on good impressions were long gone. I hope this isn't you, but if it is, it's time to snap out of it and take a good hard look at the reality of how your facility looks. If your business is great at maintaining its facility and strives to make great first impressions, nice job—keep it going!

If you haven't realized by now, I love me a good checklist. Having a great maintenance checklist will force you to not gloss over items. I've heard too many managers and owners say, "It's always been like that." No excuses allowed any more. If you want to be the best storage facility in your market, you need to treat it as such. And one of the integral components of having a truly dominant self storage business is maintaining your facility.

Take someone out with you, and walk your property. Another set of eyes will definitely help. Do a thorough walk-through of your entire facility from the drive-by approach, parking lot, office, buildings, doors, and so on. Take detailed notes on the maintenance checklist. Now, don't just write them down and move on with business as usual. Follow through on the date you will complete the necessary improvements.

3miledominators.com
Item: Maintenance Checklist

LOOK THE PART

Look The Part

For self storage businesses of all sizes, print marketing materials are a must-have. I know you may be thinking that in this Internet-driven society no one cares about brochures and business cards. If you don't have some resemblance of professional materials that speak to how you are the best in your market, then you simply won't be taken seriously. Some storage facilities spend so much time, energy, and money to be competitive. They make smart hiring decisions and build out plans to trounce the competition. But what they don't do is make the investment in marketing themselves in order to successfully sell against their competition. They miss the opportunity to deliver their value and competitive differentiators through compelling marketing materials. They miss the chance to position themselves ahead of their competitors as the obvious choice. Well, not you. Not anymore.

As an independent storage business looking to compete against the big boys, you need to look the part. Good materials can make even the smallest players look like leaders in the industry and will communicate superiority and competitive differentiation.

Storage managers need tools if they're going to be effective. Having professional materials will give your managers the resources they need to be effective in setting up alliances and referrals and stand out when it comes to those potential renters who visit two of your competitors.

Creating these materials helps to build the manager's belief in the facility as well. The owner is making an investment in something he or she can see and touch.

To get some ideas, go to the resources link and check out some sample materials that we have put together for our clients. Go to a site such as vistaprint.com, and start off by designing a new business card for your facility, or create a referral card that you will include as part of your move-in packet materials.

3miledominators.com
Item: View Sample Print Materials

3MD Storage had professional-looking materials created that it kept at its facility specifically for those times when a potential renter came in and was "shopping around." For those few times when it didn't close the sale, it made sure the customer left with its materials in its hands. About once every other month, it gets a customer who returns with those materials. It can't help but believe those materials helped to set it apart from its competition and helped to convey a sense of professionalism to the customer who decided to choose its facility.

- **Additional Revenue Created: $600**
  0.5 additional rentals a month at $1,200 Average Lifetime Value = $600
  (0.5 × $1,200 = $600)
- **Additional Value Created: $7,500**
  $600 additional revenue on an 8 Cap
  ($600 ÷ 0.08 = $7,500)

I LOVE BEING AUDITED

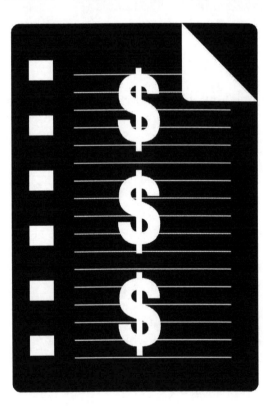

I Love Being Audited

The wonderful thing about self storage is that you're able to manage your multimillion-dollar business with just a few people. However, it's a double-edged sword. The management of your storage business will make or break your facility. Managers have a ton of autonomy which, without being checked on, can at times wreak havoc on your facility.

Honest mistakes, poor training, tunnel vision, software issues, and normal day-to-day operations can cause issues to arise at your facility. Without completing audits, you're playing with fire. Completing frequent audits of your facility is extremely important. Some facilities do this exceptionally well. Others wouldn't know where to begin.

Spending a full day every couple of months on these items will prove to be well worth the time for any owner. You will get to know the manager better and take the time to train him when issues come up. If you don't have the time to do it yourself, hire a self storage consultant to do it for you. Consultants will probably do a much better job anyway since they are coming in as unbiased third parties.

Conducting these audits will help you increase revenue, decrease expenses, reduce your liability, and grow the value of your facility. Before we go further into this domination process, you need to know where your facility is right here, right now.

Go to resources, and print off and download your audit checklists. Complete an audit of your facility today.

Item: Audit Checklists

NO MORE FRANKENSTEIN RENTAL AGREEMENT!

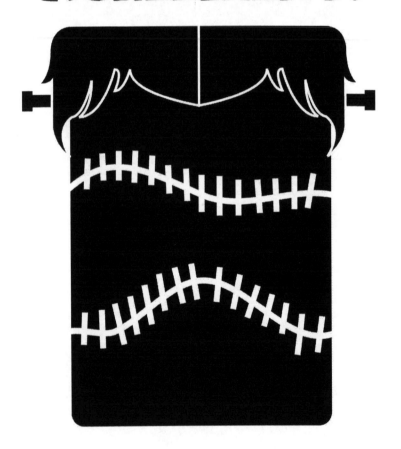

No More Frankenstein Rental Agreement

Do you want to spend a little bit of money protecting your multimillion-dollar investment, or do you want to save that money and be involved in a lawsuit? When I ask a manager or owner of a storage business when the last time was that he or she read his or her state's self storage statute or reviewed his or her rental agreement with a lawyer, I'm usually met with silence.

If you've been using the same contract for years now, you have become blind to the potential pitfalls your contract has within it. When you have a fresh pair of eyes (especially eyes that come attached to a lawyer) looking at your storage contract, you will quickly find items that must be modified to bring your contract up to the legal standards.

I've seen too many storage rental agreements that I refer to as the Frankenstein rental agreement. This is the agreement that was created by mashing together the best parts of five different agreements into what the owner now thinks is one new-and-improved document. Or even more crazy is when the property owner simply uses the placeholder agreement that has come with the storage software and figures that it's good enough!

Every one of your customers must be signing a legally solid rental agreement. This document is what stands between you losing and winning a lawsuit. It should be updated every three years because, even if your state statute hasn't changed, there is enough new case law that has occurred that should be addressed in your contract.

The bottom line is, why even put your multimillion-dollar business at risk by not having a lawyer who knows the self storage industry put a stamp of approval on your rental agreement?

Any changes you make to your contract should be in consultation with your own attorney. My advice for the best in the business is under Resources (Legal). Print off and read through your state's self storage statute. http://www.selfstorage.org/Library/Public-Library

3miledominators.com
Item: Resource Links

I LOVE IT WHEN YOU SPEAK POLICY & PROCEDURES

I Love It When You Speak Policy And Procedures

It's necessary to have a policy and procedures manual to keep your storage business running smoothly. You may have never had one before, or perhaps it's long overdue for an update. Writing an operations manual isn't difficult, but it is tedious. Write the operations manual in such a way that a stranger could walk into your office and run your business. This manual should come from the owner, consultant, management company, or even the manager with the owner's approval.

This manual should change and develop as your storage business grows. Here is a general outline to get you started:

- Store operations (opening and closing procedures, weekly and monthly procedures)
- Sales and marketing
- Selling a space
- Rental procedures
- Filing system
- Payments
- Specific questions and issues
- Security overview
- Vacating customers
- Collections and auctions
- Maintaining the property
- Legal issues

Start writing your policy and procedures manual today. Now, you won't finish this in one day, but start it and add to it continually as procedures come up during the course of your day, week, and month. Every facility is different, and you must have your manual personalized to your business operations; however, you can speed up this process by purchasing a prewritten manual in which you can then customize those parts specific to running your facility.

Item: Editable Policy And Procedures Manual

Section Two:
Leads

MARKETING IS A CONTEST FOR PEOPLE'S ATTENTION

Marketing Is A Contest For People's Attention

I'm always amazed when I ask the sites I work with what percentage of rentals they are getting as a result of drive-by or walk-in traffic. At some locations they are still receiving at least 50 percent of their rentals simply because of drive-by traffic.

So in light of seeing how many rentals are coming from people simply looking at your facility while they are in your neighborhood, I hope it's abundantly clear that you need to have your facility looking nice, professional, and approachable.

In the following pages, we will get into the details of first impressions of your site, which will include assessing your office and actually walking the property. For now, I want you to consider what a customer driving by would notice about your facility. Potential customers may have driven past your site a hundred times without ever noticing it. However, as soon as they are thinking about needing storage, it will be on their radar. Will your facility catch their eye once they have storage on their brain?

Have yourself and at least one other person get in your car and drive past your facility at least six times (three times in each direction). What jumps out at you from the road? Are there features that you could make more visible in order to attract attention?

Bonus points: Do this again, driving by at night.

3miledominators.com
Item: Drive-By Checklist

3MD Storage did two minor updates to its drive-by visibility. First, it put in brighter lights that highlighted its signage better at night. Second, it put up a simple banner that said "Storage" with an arrow pointing toward its facility. It tracked its numbers, and it saw an average of three more units renting a month from drive-by customers.

- **Additional Revenue Created: $3,600**
  3 additional rentals a month at $1,200 Average Lifetime Value
  (3 × $1,200 = $3,600)
- **Additional Value Created: $45,000**
  $3,600 additional revenue on an 8 Cap
  ($3,600 ÷ 0.08 = $45,000)

IF YOU'RE NOT A LITTLE DIFFERENT THAN YOUR COMPETITION, YOU'RE IN TROUBLE

If You're Not A Little Different From Your Competition, You're In Trouble

I could spend an entire book talking about optimization, algorithm, bounce rate, keyword density, link building, PPC, metadescription, social media, and analytics. See—I already lost you with the boring stuff!

Most of us lack the expertise, time, and patience to build a website; manage Pay-Per-Click; create social media accounts; and make sure they're optimized correctly and then, of course, marketed online correctly. Most of you will turn to those who specialize in this type of service, and you should.

Now for a word of warning: There are a lot of self storage SEO agencies and freelances now. Some are great; others are terrible.

Since most storage owners don't know how to evaluate Internet-marketing work, many SEO companies can get away with a lot. Basically, you're paying for a service without really knowing what you're paying for.

As long as you ask the right questions and pay attention to the answers, you should be able to find a self storage SEO company that makes a positive impact on your business.

Download the checklist of questions, and ask your current or potential SEO company those questions to evaluate if they will be the ones to add or remain as part of your team to dominate your local market online.

3miledominators.com
Item: Questions to ask the SEO company

3MD Storage hired a fantastic self storage SEO company whose employees were able to answer the evaluation questions and consistently deliver on what it said it would do. It tracked its leads, and it was consistently receiving an average of fifteen rentals a month from its online marketing strategies promoting its website through SEO and Google Pay-Per-Click campaigns.

- **Revenue Created: $18,000**
  15 rentals a month at $1,200 Average Lifetime Value
  (15 × $1,200 = $18,000)
- **Value Created: $225,000**
  $18,000 revenue on an 8 Cap
  ($18,000 ÷ 0.08 = $225,000)

GO WHERE THE ATTENTION IS

Go Where The Attention Is

This is always a hot topic of discussion: self storage aggregator websites. The bottom line for me when it comes to online marketing is that you must go to where the eyeballs are. Listing your facility on the aggregator websites that have a strong domain position (meaning they are found on the first page of Google) puts you in front of potential renters.

Most owners do not want a middleman between them and their prospective renters. However, it's important to realize that the exposure you are receiving on these platforms is sending you customers who wouldn't otherwise come to you directly. I feel that the customers who are going to these types of platforms would probably end up renting from one of the big boys in the industry—ones that have huge online marketing budgets and are also on the first page of Google.

I highly recommend that you choose an option that is structured as a pay-for-performance model. Meaning, the business doesn't pay the finder's fee unless that customer moves in. These aggregator platforms are investing a ton of money in having customers see their website in your local market. So you're not investing money upfront in getting seen; you only pay for the customers after they have rented from you.

It always comes back to your customer lifetime value and what you are willing to pay for a rental. You still want to have an active SEO and Pay-Per-Click strategy for your own storage business website, but being listed on these platforms simply adds to the number of people who will see your listing and give you an opportunity to rent to them, instead of going to your competition.

Call a couple of aggregator companies to get more info about their services. See the resources page online for the latest listings.

3miledominators.com
Item: Resource Links

3MD Storage listed its facility on a top aggregator website and found it was averaging an additional four rentals a month from this service.

- **Additional Revenue Created: $4,800**
  4 additional rentals a month at $1,200 Average Lifetime Value
  (4 × $1,200 = $4,800)
- **Additional Value Created: $60,000**
  $4,800 additional revenue on an 8 Cap
  ($4,800 ÷ 0.08 = $60,000)

BE THE ONE TO STAND OUT IN THE CROWD

Reviews = Rentals

Customer reviews are one of the top-ranking factors for local SEO and for turning searchers into customers. The fact is, prospective customers will nearly always read reviews and compare them to your competitor's reviews. Online reviews will definitely help you stand out and increase your rentals. No doubt about it. Self storage is a service industry, and your customers are going to do their research online to make sure they choose a facility that they can trust.

It's great to understand why getting online reviews works, but the bottom line is this: reviews = rentals. Think of it like this: having online reviews is the new word-of-mouth marketing. And I'm sure you will agree that word-of-mouth marketing is the most powerful marketing there is.

Put yourself in your potential customer's shoes. If there are multiple facilities within a three-mile radius of a customer's home, why would he or she go to a storage facility that had either a bad reputation or no reputation at all? They want their choice to be easy. Online reviews are the quickest and most trustworthy way for them to make that decision.

To trust a complete stranger with your belongings seems like a crazy idea, right? But it's what facilities ask potential customers to do every day. Good online reviews are going to give them the peace of mind that they can trust you with their possessions.

Putting an emphasis on receiving great reviews has a wonderful side effect. You will go out of your way to make sure every customer is happy with your service. And when they're not happy, you will care enough to make it right by any means necessary. At the end of the day, having that kind of mind-set, combined with a great reputation, is what's going to dominate your competition and consistently grow your sales.

1) Let's get some reviews coming in right away! Hopefully, you have been collecting e-mails from your customers as part of the rental contract process. Send an e-mail to those who have moved in during the past two months, and ask them to place a review on your Google My Business listing (provide the link to your account in the e-mail so they don't need to search for you online). To see a sample e-mail that you can cut and paste, visit the downloads link.
2) Try a one-month free trial of a self storage reviews system. Set up your reviews requests and feedback in an easy-to-use and very effective program. Call 866-510-3688 for more info.

3miledominators.com
Item: Resource Links

3MD Storage implemented a strategic system to collect and promote its customer reviews on its website, Google My Business listing, and other review sites.
Although it can't quantify exactly how many rentals came in due to those reviews, it's common sense that having the reviews helped it to stand out from its competition and compelled potential renters to call it first over its competition. It could see how having reviews easily gave it at least an additional three rentals a month.

- **Additional Revenue Created: $3,600**
  3 additional rentals a month at $1,200 Average Lifetime Value
  (3 × $1,200 = $3,600)
- **Additional Value Created: $45,000**
  $3,600 additional revenue on an 8 Cap
  ($3,600 ÷ 0.08 = $45,000)

A REFERRAL IS THE HIGHEST HONOR

★ ★ ★
★ ★

A BUSINESS CAN RECEIVE FROM A CUSTOMER

A Referral Is The Highest Honor A Business Can Receive From A Customer

Customer referrals rock as a cost-effective way to gain new rentals. We all know the magic of referrals, which offer instant credibility. Referrals are not automatic. Some just happen, but most occur because you do something to trigger them. Some storage owners assume that because their businesses are awesome, they will generate referrals by default. Not so. You must have a process in place to generate referrals for your facility.

Don't just ask customers to recommend you to others without offering them some backup. It can be as simple as supplying one of your referral business cards (yes, a specific card for referral—not just your business card) at the time of rental or giving a link to a specific page on your website. Or it could be in an e-mail sequence that goes to your current customers, describing your referral program.

Now there are many different types of incentives when it comes to referral programs. You need to decide how much you are willing to give to get the rental otherwise essentially for free, because you are not putting money into marketing to this customer. Are you willing to give the referrer twenty-five to one hundred dollars for referring someone who rents? When I factor in the lifetime value of that customer who is coming to rent from me, I know I would be happy to pay that small sum up front to the referrer if I knew on average I would be making $1,500, for example.

Along the same lines of the lifetime value of a customer, you could do a grand prize of $2,500 every six months for the customer who sends in the most referrals.

If you need a boost of rentals, this method works great, especially if your site has been around for a while. Send an e-mail to your previous and current tenants and say, "As you know, we have a referral program. Well, as we are a little bit short on our numbers this month and we are really trying to reach our goal, we need your help. We are increasing the reward for referrals to one hundred dollars for each referral. Deadline is in sixty days."

These are just some ideas to get you thinking about what you could do at your site to drive those extra rentals to your facility every month.

Spend thirty minutes to come up with some ideas on what you could offer to the referrer and to the referred customer to boost your rentals every month.

Next, send out an e-mail blast to your current customers explaining this referral program you have in place.

Finally, if you don't already, make sure you are giving everyone at the time of move-in some details about your referral program.

3miledominators.com
Item: Sample Referral Cards

3MD Storage is receiving an average of two rentals a month based on customer referrals.

- **Additional Revenue Created: $2,400**
  2 additional rentals a month at $1,200 Average Lifetime Value
  (2 × $1,200 = $2,400)
- **Additional Value Created: $30,000**
  $2,400 additional revenue on an 8 Cap
  ($2,400 ÷ 0.08 = $30,000)

JUST ONE GREAT ALLIANCE

CAN HAVE AN INCREDIBLE IMPACT ON YOUR SUCCESS.

Just One Great Alliance Can Have An Incredible Impact

I'll be the first to admit that what I'm about to propose to you may seem counterintuitive to everything we have talked about regarding dominating your competition. I don't want to come across as saying that your competitor down the street is your enemy. In fact, your competitors can be better allies than competitors. Now don't get me wrong; I want your site to be the obvious choice as the go-to self storage facility in your market, but as they say—you catch more flies with honey than you do with vinegar. In this case, you get more rentals by having competitor alliances and paying a referral fee than by being looked at as the enemy.

Step 1: Go back and refer to your spreadsheet where you listed all of your competitors with their features and availability (you did that, right?). The goal here is to find what you offer that your competition doesn't, and vice versa: amenities such as climate control, RV spaces, and so on.

Step 2: Decide on what you will give. Just like a regular referral, what are you paying for customer referrals? Again, keep in mind the average lifetime customer value. Does offering a hundred dollars as a referral reward, for example, seem too much when considering how much an average rental will bring to your facility?

Step 3: I recommend visiting your competition and getting to know them. Introduce yourself. You have plenty in common already by both of you being in the storage industry. Don't jump right into setting up an alliance on day one. Create this relationship organically. Just stop in, and get a feel for your competition and how things are going for them. Now, some will be cold as ice and not want anything to do with you. Fine. Move on. There are plenty of self storage sites in your area that will be cool with you stopping by to say hi.

Step 4: After a week or so, send those who were nice to you a letter in the mail. An e-mail is too impersonal, and trust me, a letter will leave a great impression. Basically, let them know it was great to get to know them and that you want to present an offer that would be of mutual benefit. An example of such a letter is found at the resource link.

Step 5: After waiting a couple of days after the letter should have arrived, go back to say hi and see if they have received your letter, and go over any details.

You may be asking yourself, why does this work? Well, there is a reward in it for the other manager in the form of the referral money. It works for him or her because he or she is still able to provide value to a customer without simply saying he or she can't help you and hanging up the phone. And of course it works for you because you get the rental.

Now this isn't totally one sided. If your competition has inventory available that you do not or you simply don't have something that your customer is looking for (like climate control), let your competitor alliance know that you will be returning the favor as well.

Tip: Here is the best way to make sure the lead is transferred in the most efficient way to ensure that this storage lead is followed up on. Do not just say, "Here is the other facility's phone number." Instead ask for the customer's contact info and then have your competitor alliance call the customer directly.

Go back to your competition spreadsheet, and map out what days you will make the time to go and introduce yourself. Simply strike up a conversation. You obviously have a ton in common by both being self storage managers.

Then the same day that you meet with them, write them a letter that you will be mailing a week later (Step 4).

Go to resources to download scripts and steps to follow.

3miledominators.com
Item: Competition Alliance Letter

3MD Storage set up two competitor alliances, and each alliance sends on average one customer each month.

- **Additional Revenue Created: $2,400**
  2 additional rentals a month at $1,200 Average Lifetime Value
  (2 × $1,200 = $2,400)
- **Additional Value Created: $30,000**
  $2,400 additional revenue on an 8 Cap
  ($2,400 ÷ 0.08 = $30,000)

We Have A Lot In Common

Forming alliances with the surrounding businesses in your market will be a huge advantage for your self storage business.

Base your criteria for forming these alliances on who will have a high likelihood of needing storage (such as apartments and condos, realtors, moving companies, and retirement centers). But another rule of thumb is that there will be a percentage of people visiting your neighborhood businesses that need storage (like those in a coffee shop). Remember, one out of every ten people in your neighborhood are using storage! By putting forth some effort in marketing materials and going out on a schedule to establish these alliances, your business will rule your market simply because your competition didn't have this strategy as a focus for its business.

Imagine having fifty other surrounding businesses promoting your facility in some way, shape, or form six months from now. That would have a crazy impact on your business. It takes work. But anything with big rewards takes work.

Here is an example using an apartment complex: according to Self-Storage Almanac, 27 percent of storage renters live in an apartment or condo. So it's obvious you need to be marketing and forming alliances with apartments and condos to bring in a steady stream of rentals each month.

Visit the complexes first to simply introduce yourself as the manager of your storage facility. Do not ask to set up an alliance with them at this time. (I recommend this for all of your target alliances.) Ask what they have as materials you can put on your office bulletin board or coupon move-in packets that you could give to your rental customers who would benefit from them and could possibly bring new business to the alliance you're looking to set up.

Here's an example of what to say: "Hi, my name is Jim with My Storage. We're just down the street, and I'm thinking that we probably do business with a lot of the same people. I was wondering if you had any coupons, menus, business cards, or something that I can include in my new move-in packets or display in my storage rental office." So the difference is, rather than asking for something, you are giving them something first.

Now you can go back a week or so later to those who provided you with apartment or condo materials (or coupons from their business—you get the idea) and show them the materials that you have for them. Most people are decent human beings, and they will in turn have no problem helping you out as well. Then at that point, you can explain your strategic alliance program and form that partnership. Go to the resources link to view some images to get an idea. The goal is to make it personalized to the facility you are working with.

Those places that agree to give you a display on their counter or to put your storage materials in their own move-in packets are now valued allies; make sure their friendliness does not go unrewarded. Send them a thank-you card with a gift card for dinner and a movie. It doesn't have to be big, but it will leave a great impression, and they will be more willing to follow through on your alliance.

As far as what you will be giving as a referral fee, we go back to what that rental is worth to you and what you are willing to give as a reward for them sending business to you. I've seen anywhere from twenty-five to one hundred dollars. Money talks—the higher the referral fee, the more likely you will be top of mind as they push your storage business to their renters.

Google and list every one of the apartment complexes and condominiums in your alliance spreadsheet. Create a schedule to visit, and present your materials to them. A great goal to set is to create two apartment alliances each week. You will see when you download the spreadsheet that there are other categories and schedules of alliances to set up as well, but I suggest to start off with apartment complexes to make the best use of your time and to get rentals from this source flowing right away.

3miledominators.com
Items: Alliance Spreadsheet, Sample Alliance Materials

3MD Storage located ten apartment complexes within a three-mile radius of its facility. The manager was able to set up an alliance with three of them. Those three alliances sent it an average of two rentals a month.

- **Additional Revenue Created: $2,400**
  2 additional rentals a month at $1,200 Average Lifetime Value
  (2 × $1,200 = $2,400)
- **Additional Value Created: $30,000**
  $2,400 additional revenue on an 8 Cap
  ($2,400 ÷ 0.08 = $30,000)

Section Three:
Rentals

IF THEY LIKE YOU THEY WILL LISTEN. IF THEY LISTEN THEY WILL BELIEVE. IF THEY BELIEVE THEY WILL BUY.

If They Believe, They Will Buy

Every call counts! Executing a great sales call that stands out from your competition and compels the person on the other side of that phone to act and rent from you is the foundation of having a successful self storage business.

You're spending money to attract customers to pick up the phone and rent from you. But you're wasting your advertising dollars if the manager has a terrible sales presentation, basically encouraging that potential customer to call the next facility down the road.

It only takes a few minutes to perform an excellent sales call versus taking the same amount of time and blowing the sale. I've secret shopped too many self storage properties to count over the years, and I'm still amazed how many storage facilities are absolutely terrible on the phone or, even worse, don't answer the phone at all.

Draw a line in the sand today, and let it be known that you will not have a subpar phone sales presentation ever again. Because if you don't, nothing in this book will matter. It will all go to waste if you don't have a fantastic phone sales presentation to back it up.

It will be too much to put the sales script here, plus I'm always updating and tweaking the sales presentation to be the best and most memorable. Go to the resources page to download and customize it for your facility. But I want you to go through the following actions today. Today is all about preparing to construct the best sales presentation your facility has ever had.

1) Go to resources link and download the sales scripts that you will be customizing for your facility. Here I will break down each section of the sales presentation and explain why the phrasing and structure is so important. Read it out loud. Listen to sample recorded sales calls.

2) Take out a sheet of paper and spend thirty minutes: on one side list all of the features of your facility and on the other side, the benefits of each feature. For example, we have coded gate access so that we can properly monitor those who come and go on the property. Another example is that we have drive-up access so customers don't have to worry about hiking upstairs. Be specific. You will make a much better impression, and it will make a big difference in your sales presentation.

3) You should have already done this recently, but while you are in sales-call mode, call back and secret shop your competition over the phone. If you put yourself in your customer's shoes, you will quickly see how you can give a sales presentation that will blow everyone else away and compel your potential customer to rent from you.

Item: Sales Scripts

3MD Storage is averaging forty-five phone rental inquiries every month. Its conversion percentage was 73 percent. Focusing on improving its sales-call presentation, it was able to increase its conversion to 83 percent. So, rather than closing thirty-three of its forty-five rental inquiries (73 percent), it is now renting to thirty-seven of those same forty-five inquiries (83 percent). That is an extra 4 rentals each month by simply having a more effective sales presentation.

- **Additional Revenue Created: $4,800**
  4 additional rentals a month at $1,200 Average
  Lifetime Value
  (4 x $1,200 = $4,800)
- **Additional Value Created: $60,000**
  $4,800 additional revenue on an 8 Cap
  ($4,800 ÷ 0.08 = $60,000)

YOU NEED TO GIVE PEOPLE A REASON TO CHOOSE YOUR BUSINESS

You Need To Give People A Reason To Choose Your Business

When it comes to what discounts and specials you should have for your facility, there are a variety of factors to consider. What is your occupancy? Are you a newly opened facility and in rent-up mode? Are you in a highly competitive market where everyone is offering huge move-in specials? If your conversions are high and you don't need to offer a move-in special, then that is great. However, more often than not, some sort of discount or special is necessary to spur action from the customer to take the next step to come to your facility to rent.

I've seen some successful storage businesses have the luxury of not being in a highly competitive market but still want to give something to the customer to compel them to come down to visit their site. In those instances, at the end of the phone sales presentation, they simply say, "If you come down today, we have a couple of free vouchers for (insert gift—Amazon gift card, local restaurant gift card, and so on) that we would give you to come take a tour."

But most of us are competing with the big boys in the industry, and we must raise our game when it comes to move-in specials and discounts. In my experience, I have no problem in offering a highly competitive move-in special because, again, I understand the average lifetime customer value. The entire point of marketing and sales is to get the rental. If that means you must give up a month of rent to do so, by all means do it! I'm not saying you have to give away the farm here. In fact, I'll be the first to advise you to give away the least amount possible to acquire a customer. But if the math works out, giving away a month of rent or even two months of rent to acquire a customer will put way more money into your bank account than not having any renters because you're too scared or proud to give a decent offer.

The question you must ask yourself is this: What are you willing to give up front in order to gain that customer?

Another aspect of having a dominating sales-call presentation is creating and offering your USP (Unique Selling Proposition). Basically, this will give your call a little extra spice and be very memorable to your caller. Be bold, be different, and by all means, don't copy everybody else. Some examples can be
- satisfaction guarantee;
- free rental truck;
- free moving-in supply (lock and boxes).

1) Take a few minutes to brainstorm all the different specials, discounts, and giveaways you could offer to stand out and compel people to rent from you. Again, if you're making calls to your competition, you should know what kind of specials your competitors are offering.
2) Take a few more minutes and brainstorm some USPs that you can offer during your call to really stand out from the crowd.

3miledominators.com
Item: Sample USP List

By mentioning its USP of a free moving-in supply that consisted of a free disc lock, two small boxes, and two large boxes (their cost: $10.69), 3MD Storage was able to compel two more renters each month to rent from it rather than from its competition.

- **Additional Revenue Created: $2,400**
  2 additional rentals a month at $1,200 Average
  Lifetime Value
  (2 × $1,200 = $2,400)
- **Additional Value Created: $30,000**
  $2,400 additional revenue on an 8 Cap
  ($2,400 ÷ 0.08 = $30,000)

DON'T TALK, ACT DON'T SAY, SHOW DON'T PROMISE, PROVE

Don't Talk, Act. Don't Say, Show. Don't Promise, Prove.

Having a proper follow-up system in place can have a profound impact on your storage business. A follow-up phone call to a potential renter who has already shown interest in renting from you is a crucial aspect of closing the sale. Many businesses either neglect it or do not have an established plan. The first step is to have a means of reaching the customer either through e-mail or by phone. In the sales script, you have seen that this step of getting a customer's contact info is built into the sales presentation.

When following up, contact the customer with a reason that moves the sales process along. Don't just call or e-mail to ask if he or she has made up his or her mind, although that is still more than what most of your competition will do! Instead you should have a sequence that looks something like this:

1) Immediately after the sales call, send him or her an e-mail giving him or her a quote of what you discussed. A template can easily be created so that you just need to fill in the specifics such as size, price, and specials. The rest of the e-mail can be from a reusable template that has the features and benefits of your facility and some testimonials. This establishes that you truly appreciate the customer for reaching out to you and begins to establish the trust factor that is necessary in getting the rental.

2) Put reminders in your online calendar or some other system that works for you to contact him or her back when he or she said he or she would be in need of storage. Follow up with him or her again before that time to reestablish a connection, and offer any new specials or discounts that you could give to him or her to get the rental. Again, don't just call to ask if he or she needs storage. If he or she hasn't already reserved a unit with you, it's time to sweeten the deal

with a "new" special that you are running that you thought could really benefit him or her.

Follow-ups demonstrate your determination to build a relationship with your customer and to build the rapport and trust for them to agree that you are the self storage facility for them. Doing some simple follow-up is much more cost effective than chasing down new customers.

Go to the resources link and model the first follow-up e-mail template. We have a system that makes the design look great and puts your customers in an automatic follow-up sequence for you, but you can also design a basic version today that you can start using on your very next sales call.

3miledominators.com
Item: Sample Follow-Up E-mail

3MD Storage implemented a follow-up system. In the first month, it saw its conversions go up an extra 7 percent! Of the forty-five calls it received the prior month, that 7 percent boost equated to an extra three rentals that month!

- **Additional Revenue Created: $3,600**
  3 additional rentals a month at $1,200 Average Lifetime Value
  (3 × $1,200 = $3,600)
- **Additional Value Created: $45,000**
  $3,600 additional revenue on an 8 Cap
  ($3,600 ÷ 0.08 = $45,000)

EVERY CALL COUNTS!

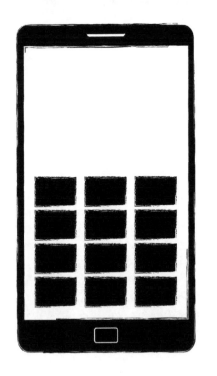

Every Call Counts!

You're paying real cash to make that phone of yours ring. Yet I guarantee you're not answering every call that is coming in. I get it. You won't always be able to answer the phone every time it rings because it's after hours, you're cleaning a unit, you're at lunch, you're on the other line, you're renting or showing a unit—the list goes on and on. How often do potential customers leave a message when they don't reach a live person? Not very often. They want answers to their questions now, not later when it's convenient for you.

Having a call center as a partner in answering those calls that would have gone to voice mail is extremely valuable. I've seen time and time again the moment a facility has plugged in a call center to help with those calls they were missing, they immediately see a bump in rentals. In some instances it can be shocking how many calls were going unanswered. I remember those days when I was a manager and the phone hadn't rang the entire day, but the second I was in a position to not answer the phone—it rang. That's just how it seems to work out.

When you weigh the monthly cost of a call center versus the cost of losing a rental because you were not able to give a sales presentation, it's clear that this is a service you need at your facility. In fact, most, if not all, call centers today will provide you with the reports in black and white about how many calls they took, how many sales presentations were given, and how many reservations they placed for your facility.

I understand that the call center reps may not be giving the sales presentation exactly as we have outlined. But you can definitely instruct them on specifics of your site, specials, and so on. Most call centers are very professional, and their workers get a lot of practice every single day giving many sales presentations. I'm more comfortable in having a call center employee give a basic sales presentation than in risking a potential customer's not leaving a message or not answering the phone on a callback.

Call three call centers today to get a quote for their services. Some storage software even provide support specifically for their clients on their platforms. Try a call center for one month, and then analyze the reports that show its activity for your business.

3miledominators.com

Item: Vendor Links

After a month of using a call center, 3MD Storage saw the call center gave an additional ten sales presentations that would have otherwise been missed. Of those ten presentations, six rented.

- **Additional Revenue Created: $7,200**
  6 additional rentals a month at $1,200 Average Lifetime Value
  (6 × $1,200 = $7,200)
- **Additional Value Created: $90,000**
  $7,200 additional revenue on an 8 Cap
  ($7,200 ÷ 0.08 = $90,000)

YOU NEVER GET A SECOND CHANCE

TO MAKE A GREAT FIRST IMPRESSION

You Never Get A Second Chance To Make A Great First Impression

Looks matter. When your facility is clean and professional looking, it will help put your potential customers in a state of mind to rent from you even before they walk into your office. Rather than going through the entire list of items to look for here, I would definitely urge you to go through the maintenance checklist on the resources page. However, some obvious items to address immediately are as follows: How's your signage looking? Do you have signage on your gate that welcomes your customers and clearly gives the gate and office hours and contact number? Is it time to repaint your curbs? Is your landscaping looking sharp? Are the parking stripes clear? A creative sign I once saw at a facility at the parking place right by the office door read "We Love Our Customers."

The key is to be asking yourself what you can do to improve upon the look of your facility to put a customer in the right frame of mind before he or she even walks into your office.

Walk around with another person, and point out what could be improved upon to help potential customers decide that your facility is the place for them before they even walk into your office.

3miledominators.com
Item: First-impression Checklist

YOUR OFFICE IS A DIRECT REFLECTION OF YOUR FACILITY

Your Office is A Direct Reflection Of Your Facility

When a potential customer walks in your office doors, it's obvious you want to make a great first impression. Your office is a direct reflection of the pride you take in running and maintaining your facility.

I've been in offices that are the size of a broom closet and others that are big enough to play a football game in. The size doesn't matter—what matters is how professional it looks. From secret shopping many storage businesses in my day, here is a brief list of what not to have in your office: clutter, stacks and stacks of paperwork, pets, your kids running around, and maintenance equipment in corners; the list goes on, but you get the idea.

What's great about this is that it doesn't take much time or money to put together an office that makes a positive impression on your customers:

- The office smells nice.
- The manager is dressed professionally.
- The desk and counter are clean and orderly.
- A security display is in the front and center.
- The merchandise display is properly stocked and set up (more on this later).
- There is cold water or hot coffee to offer your customers.

Download the office-setup checklist to get ideas on how you can improve upon your current office setup.

3miledominators.com
Item: Office-setup checklist

3MD Storage was able to convert an additional two rentals from those shopping around by creating a professional office that conveyed cleanliness, order, and security.

- **Additional Revenue Created: $2,400**
  2 additional rentals a month at $1,200 Average Lifetime Value
  (2 × $1,200 = $2,400)
- **Additional Value Created: $30,000**
  $2,400 additional revenue on an 8 Cap
  ($2,400 ÷ 0.08 = $30,000)

HUSTLE AND HEART WILL SET YOU APART

HUSTLE AND HEART WILL SET YOU APART

When showing a potential customer a unit at your facility, there is so much more you can do than just going out, rolling up the unit door, and saying, "Well, there it is."

While going out to show the customer the size that you believe will best fit his or her needs, showcase your facility. Demonstrating the features and benefits of your facility while showing a unit to a potential customer doesn't take any more time but will definitely demonstrate that your facility is the one to rent from.

If you have a golf cart (and I hope you do) to bring potential customers to the unit, make sure it is clean! It drives me crazy when I secret shop a facility and they take me out to see a unit, and I'm taken out in a golf cart that is full of maintenance items and a smelly garbage can and is just grimy. When you are not using your golf cart for maintenance duties, have it primed and ready to take customers to and from the unit.

While going to the unit, make it a point to say that you take pride in your facility. Tell them about how long you have been in the self storage business or what brought you to the industry. If you see something on the ground, pick it up. Point out the security cameras to emphasize that your facility is secure—that they can trust you with their items.

As you roll up the unit door, talk about how you maintain each unit so they don't need to worry about it functioning; talk about the partitions, pest control, and so on. Demonstrate to them how to properly secure the unit with the latch and lock. I can't tell you how many times new renters have locked their unit open, thinking that it was secured.

Your actual unit most likely doesn't look any different from the place down the street; however, the place down the street isn't educating the customer why you do what you do and why your place is the obvious choice.

On the way back to the office, demonstrate how the coded gate works and, again, stress how your facility provides security by monitoring who is entering and exiting the property.

Starting today, incorporate these items into your sales presentation.

Item: Sales Presentation

3MD Storage began a much smoother and more professional sales presentation while showing a potential renter a unit. It has seen that it has increased its in-person conversions by at least one additional rental a month.

- **Additional Revenue Created: $1,200**
  1 additional rental a month at $1,200 Average Lifetime Value
  (1 × $1,200 = $1,200)
- **Additional Value Created: $15,000**
  $1,200 additional revenue on a 8 CAP
  ($1,200 ÷ 0.08 = $15,000)

SET YOURSELF UP FOR SUCCESS

Set Yourself Up For Success

You will never have a better time to set yourself up for success than when you have a new customer standing in front of you.

What do I mean by success? I mean gathering a testimonial, getting referral cards in his or her hands, setting up on autopay, and so on. Let's show some examples during a typical move-in.

Autopay

While signing the rental contract, ask the customer, "What card would you like to put on your account to put your unit on autopay so you don't ever have to worry about any late fees?" Don't ask if he or she would like to go on autopay. Form the question as a part of the rental process of having his or her account on autopay. This simple approach will boost your autopay percentage, which is golden—customers who are on autopay and don't have to be reminded every month to pay their storage bill will stay longer.

Video Testimonial

I love having a promotional item about our customer video testimonials on the counter next to where renters are signing the contract. I love putting video testimonials of our customers on the business website and YouTube, as social proof that we are the best in town. Remember, YouTube is owned by Google, and at times these testimonial videos come up under search results when customers are looking for storage. I casually ask the customers if they wouldn't mind giving a quick video testimonial of the facility and why they chose us. In return, I would happily give them a free lock, ten dollars off moving supplies, no admin fee, and so on. You don't need a ton, but having some great testimonials from happy customers will definitely help you for future rentals when people are on your website and see that social proof that you are the best!

Extended Hours

As they are filling out the paperwork on the rental agreement, ask if they would be interested in extended hours for fifteen dollars a month. You get an instant revenue boost by simply identifying customers who need that service.

Merchandise Sales

There will never be a better time to sell merchandise than during the time of move-in. I have an entire section dedicated to merchandise sales in the revenue-management section of this book.

How They Found You

At the time of move-in, you must make sure to find out how they found your facility, and document it accordingly. Put it in your ROI console and also in your self storage software for accurate reporting. Gathering this information for each and every rental is crucial to the success of your current and future marketing.

Move-In Packet Materials

Be professional and have move-in packets ready to go. The last thing a customer wants to do is to wait while you're putting documents and materials together. Here are some items to put in your move-in packet:
- Customer move-in envelope
- Rental agreement
- Company brochure
- Business card
- Insurance brochure
- Insurance addendum
- New tenant questionnaire
- Gate code instruction card
- Change-of-address card
- Referral-program cards
- Monthly credit-card billing authorization form

About referral cards—this is the perfect time to go over your referral program and supply them with some referral cards.

With your very next rental, start the autopay strategy, ask for a video testimonial, ask if they are interested in extended hours, ask what moving supplies they will need, and of course how they found you.

3miledominators.com

Item: Samples of move-in materials and displays

Section Four:
Revenue Management

$$$

SHOW ME THE MONEY!

$$$

Show Me The Money!

Revenue management is obviously an extremely important part of running a successful and profitable self storage business. I see too many owners who get caught up in paralysis by analysis and never really get their revenue-management systems in place consistently.

I like to keep things simple.

There are only three ways to grow your storage business:

1) Get rentals.
2) Increase the value of each customer.
3) Lower operating expenses and increase margins.

If you think about it, you'll realize that everything you've done to increase profits has fallen under one of those three categories.

In the next few pages, let's get into some simple but very effective revenue-management strategies that you can easily implement right away to start seeing financial benefits.

Write down the amount of rentals you averaged in the past 12 months.

Now increase the amount of rentals by 10 percent. Write that down.

Write down your average rental rate.

Now increase the average rental rate by 10 percent. Write that down.

Write down the total average monthly operating expenses?

Now decrease the monthly operating expenses by 5 percent. Write that down.

These numbers by themselves may not sound like much, but put them all together, and that is a 25 percent increase to your storage business.

3miledominators.com
Item: 3 Ways To Grow

GOOD
BETTER
BEST

Good, Better, Best

This will be short but very effective in increasing your revenue. It's a simple strategy that I don't see very often: the Good, Better, Best pricing model.

For example, instead of having all of your 10 x 20s at a single price point, this multiprice strategy allows customers to choose which price and unit locations work best for them. Now, when quoting the unit price online and on the phone, quote the lowest price. But when the customer is at your facility and taking the tour, then explain to them the difference in pricing if it's something that would benefit them.

Examples of units that can be priced higher than your normal units could be temperature control (of course), corner units that make it easier to get in and out of, units by an elevator, units with electricity, and so on.

Do a walk-through of your facility, and mark those units that you could raise the standard rates on to create some good, better, and best unit options.

3miledominators.com
Item: Good, Better, Best

3MD Storage was able to locate thirty units at its property that it could charge higher prices on than the rest of the units in that size. It averaged a twenty-dollar increase per unit with this pricing model. This equated to an extra $600 a month in income.

- **Additional Revenue Created: $7,200**

    30 units averaged $20 per space increase (30 × $20 = $600).

    $600 monthly increase at 12 month average stay ($600 × 12 = $7,200)

- **Additional Value Created: $90,000**

    $7,200 additional revenue on an 8 Cap ($7,200 ÷ 0.08 = $90,000)

RAISING RATES -

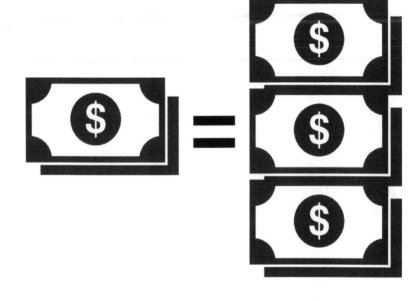

JUST DO IT!

Raising Rates—Just Do It!

There is no one-size-fits-all revenue-management model; however, I've found that simply having a structure in place that you can then modify as you see fit will put you light-years ahead of where you would be without any revenue model at all.

Nothing causes more debate, fear, and confusion than revenue management. But nothing is more important to the financial success of your self storage investment.

There are only two ways to raise your rates: (1) increase your street rates or (2) increase the rates of existing customers paying below street rate.

Let's make this simple.

Increase Your Street Rates
Increase your street rates by 8 percent whenever your occupancy of that size code has reached 90 percent or higher for at least ninety days. It's simple. If you're 100 percent occupied, you are losing money!

Increase the Rates of Existing Customers (Regardless of Your Occupancy)
Increase customers' rates 8 percent six months after move-in and 8 percent every nine months after that. Cap the increase so that they will not pay more than 20 percent above the current street rate.

Now, thankfully, if your storage software is any good, you will be able to put in these guidelines and have the rate increases occur automatically and, most importantly, consistently! The idea of raising rates is usually met with fear that everyone will move out. After all these years, I've never had a mass move-out. Just a little complaining and a lot more money.

Go into your storage software, and program your rate increases automatically using the numbers above as a guideline. Just do it!

On average, 3MD Storage brings in an additional $350 a month from scheduled rate increases of existing customers.

- **Additional Revenue Created: $4,200**
  $350 additional revenue each month. The average customer stays 12 months.
  (350 × $12 = $4,200)
- **Additional Value Created: $52,500**
  $4,200 additional revenue on an 8 Cap
  ($4,200 ÷ 0.08 = $52,500)

TENANT INSURANCE = WIN WIN

Tenant Insurance = Win-Win

Most, if not all, of the industry big boys now require customers to have tenant insurance coverage, and many operators are doing the same.

Offering a tenant insurance program can be very beneficial to customers and your storage business. Having tenant insurance removes the responsibility from the managers to "fix it" when a loss occurs. Even though your lease states that you're not responsible for damage to tenant property, angry customers will still do what they can to make your life miserable.

But let's get to the real reason you want to be offering a tenant insurance program at your facility: the revenue that it generates. When properly implemented, a program will generally generate more revenue than truck rentals or merchandise sales.

You really have nothing to lose by offering tenant insurance. That's it. Simple as that. Nothing more to say. Get it and implement a program now.

Call at least three of the tenant insurance providers from the resources link, and ask the following questions:
- What training will be provided?
- What is my commission?
- What marketing materials will be provided?
- Who will answer my questions if my customers or I need support?
- Who will assist me in reaching out to my existing tenant base?
- What will be the out-of-pocket cost to enroll current tenants?
- Do I need a limited license to sell insurance?

3MD Storage averages eighteen new customer insurance policies each month, paying them a four dollar commission for each policy each month (18 × $4 = $72 per month).

- **Additional Revenue Created: $864**
  18 policies paying $4 each and the average stay is 12 months
  (18 × $4 = $72) ($72 × 12 = $864)
- **Additional Value Created: $10,800**
  $864 additional revenue on a 8 CAP
  ($864 ÷ 0.08 = $10,800)

I Need Storage Now!

All storage managers experience it. They have potential renters who walk through their doors saying they need a unit. These interested customers have not looked online or have not talked to the manager previously.

These renters are the type of people who just need a unit right now. They are in front of you now, ready to rent. Once the manager has established that this potential renter has not had any prior exposure to your facility, it's time to take him or her through your sales process. The only change will be that when you quote the prices of the units, mark them all up by 15 percent.

The customer saw your facility, walked into your door, you showed them why you're the best. It won't take much of a sales process. They need the space—now!

It's common practice for storage locations to list their prices for their units lower online than what their standard rates are. They do this because the competition is so heavy online and the competition is only a mouse click away. However, when you have a customer ready to buy in front of you right then and there, the managers should have the flexibility to charge a premium on those units for such walk-in customers.

Create a walk-in price 15 percent higher than your standard prices for your vacant units. Try this technique for the next month to see for yourself that this strategy works and that it's like an immediate rate increase.

3miledominators.com
Item: Walk-In Pricing

3MD Storage began charging a 15 percent higher rate for walk-in customers. After tracking this for the first month, it saw that it rented four units to walk-in customers and charged on average fifteen dollars higher than the standard rates on those units.

- **Additional Revenue Created: $720**
  4 rentals at an increase of $15 per unit. Average length of stay is 12 months.
  (4 × $15 = $60) ($60 × 12 = $720)
- **Additional Value Created: $9,000**
  $720 additional revenue on an 8 Cap
  ($720 ÷ 0.08 = $9,000)

BE A
ONE
STOP
SHOP

Be A One-Stop Shop

Retail sales go hand in hand with the self storage business. It's a very important part of the revenue-management strategy.

First off, get your merchandise display in order. What you do to create a retail look and feel shows your customer that you want to provide him or her what he or she needs to make his or her move easier, which will bring in additional income. From small to large offices, there are some great ways to professionally display your merchandise. Go to the resources page to see some sample planograms, which are predesigned sketches outlining which items go where.

Get it out of your head that the retail prices at the big-box stores or home-improvement stores are so cheap that you can't compete. You're not competing. Your business is storage. You offer locks, boxes, and so on as a convenience to your customers. How many of your customers even know how much a lock costs? Even if they did, not many would go out of their way to save a couple of bucks.

I strongly recommend requiring that your facility only allows disc locks or cylinder locks, depending on your hasp. Letting customers use whatever lock they like brings on a host of problems when they use little combination locks that are a target for the criminal type. You're doing your customers a favor by requiring them to have the best lock to secure their goods.

Offer packing "kits" for one, two, or more rooms. The suggestions in a kit make decisions much easier for your customer. Many times your supplier will have information and even the printed materials to showcase these kits.

Customers are often hesitant to purchase a large number of boxes, even bundles, as they're just not sure how many they're really going to need. Take that worry away by offering to buy back any flat, unmarked, ready-for-retail boxes purchased but never used. This works well to increase bundle sales as well.

Finally, make sure you have a good sign, visible from the street, to catch drive-by customers who don't have storage but who do need some boxes. Again, your supplier will have a nice display to use.

By simply having a more focused approach to merchandise sales, you will see that number go higher and higher, because it will become a part of your sales process during a rental.

Call your supplier, and ask for a planogram to fit your space. This will help you to properly display your products. They should do this for you for free since the more you sell, the more they sell.

3miledominators.com
Item: Vendor Links

3MD Storage really focused on increasing its average merchandise sale per rental. It was steadily able to increase its monthly merchandise sales from $400 a month to $700 a month.

- **Additional Revenue Created: $3,600**
  It averaged this additional income throughout the year.
  ($300 × 12 = $3,600)
- **Additional Value Created: $45,000**
  $3,600 additional revenue on an 8 Cap
  ($3,600 ÷ 0.08 = $45,000)

Truck Rental—Visibility, Occupancy, Revenue

Most people need some kind of truck to move things into storage, so why not bring value to your customers by offering that service? Offering a truck rental service will be another way to differentiate you from your competition. It also can help your facility's visibility, occupancy, and revenue. For instance, if your location does not receive much drive-by traffic, and you have a branded truck, it can be placed somewhere with high visibility. In addition, a truck rental can give you the flexibility to offer the free use of a truck instead of a free month of rent as an inducement to customers.

Some facilities buy their own truck, others rent, and others have a simple commission relationship with a company such as U-Haul. I personally don't want to have the responsibility for maintenance or liability, so I like the commission partnership with truck rental services.

Call some services under the resources section to get more info about adding a truck rental service.

3miledominators.com
Item: Vendor Links

3MD Storage has been averaging $800 in truck rental commissions each month.

- **Additional Revenue Created: $9,600 over the course of a year**

  ($800 × 12 = $9,600)
- **Additional Value Created: $120,000**

  $9,600 additional revenue on an 8 Cap

  ($9,600 ÷ 0.08 = $120,000)

OUT WITH THE BAD IN WITH THE GOOD

Out With The Bad, In With The Good

Let's put some systems in place to keep collections to a minimum and release those nonpaying units for rental to someone who will pay.

First off, make it easy for your customer to pay you. Accept cash, checks, credit cards, and debit cards. Two must-haves that will minimize the amount of customers who are late: have online bill pay on your website, and push as many customers as possible to sign up for autopay at the time of the rental.

Use technology to your advantage. The main storage software already have integrated systems in place to help you collect your monthly rent from customers and to synchronize with your gate to lock late customers out. These systems can automatically send e-mails, and send automated calls and text messages. I personally love the text message feature. Everyone screens their phone calls, and e-mails are becoming less and less of a priority for people to read, but everyone still reads and responds to text messages!

No matter what systems you put into place to minimize the amount of people who are late in paying their rent, there is always going to be that percentage of people who will move into lien status. Move your lien process along as quickly as your statutes will allow. We all hate it when we have a unit size that is in high demand but there is a customer in that size that is late and, chances are, may not ever pay. Too often I see the situation where the facility wants to wait until it has a certain number of units to make an auction worth it. What does that mean? You're burning money as long as those units are sitting there not bringing in revenue!

Set up an aggressive late-fee schedule. Make sure this schedule is clear in your lease by explaining exactly how many days late the following will occur: gate lockout, unit overlock, late fees, auction preparation fee, auction fee, and so on. Check with your state statutes to make sure you're following regulations, or consult with an attorney familiar with your state statutes.

3miledominators.com
Item: Resource Links

BEWARE OF LITTLE EXPENSES. A SMALL LEAK WILL SINK A GREAT SHIP.

A Small Leak Will Sink A Great Ship

I'm all for saving money, but you must know what is a necessary expense that is bringing in revenue and supporting your business versus an expense that is useless and can be reduced or eliminated.

The key to making these decisions is knowing exactly what you're paying for. When was the last time you truly went through your profit and loss statement? When was the last time you examined every invoice that was paid? It's amazing what can be accomplished when just a little bit of time and energy is focused on compiling this information.

Once you have the documents in hand, before cutting an expense, ask yourself the following questions:

- Will cutting this expense reduce my ability to compete effectively?
- Will cutting this expense reduce the quality of my business?
- Will cutting this expense negatively impact my customer's experience with my company?

If the answer to all of these questions is no, then you can probably cut the expense and feel good about it. If the answer to any of these questions is yes, you'd better be very careful and ask yourself the following question: Can I get this item less expensively or perform the activity more cost-effectively?

Pull the past twelve months' profit and loss report and invoices. Ask yourself those questions for each item, and then take the necessary action.

3miledominators.com
Item: Expense Checklist

Section Five:
Domination

YOUR MANAGER WILL MAKE OR BREAK YOUR BUSINESS

Your Manager Will Make Or Break Your Business

Having the right manager for your self storage business is one of the most, if not the most, important factors for the success of your property. Your manager will make or break your facility.

I can't tell you how many times I've seen that a manager has gotten the job because he or she is a friend of the owner or a relative of the previous manager. It's amazing that some owners will hand over the keys of their multimillion-dollar investment to someone because it is convenient.

Take your time to find the right manager for your property. When the decision is rushed, more often than not you're back to square one looking for a new manager in a short period of time.

I highly recommend going through an in-depth interview process. Luckily, I have a fantastic manager-hiring system that I call the flake filter: it presents to you quality candidates on a silver platter (see the action icon below)!

Training for this position is extremely important, and it makes everything so much easier when you are starting from a strong foundation of great character and a healthy dose of common sense. Everything else can be trained when it comes to sales, marketing, customer service, and the rest of what comes along with being a self storage manager.

Go to the resource page and view the manager-hiring system that you can easily model and use the next time you are in need of a strong and capable self storage manager.

Item: Manager-Hiring System

A few years back, 3MD Storage was trying to figure out why rentals and income had steadily declined. It remained this way for way too long. Finally, after seeing the manager wasn't taking pride in the job, sales evaluations were slipping, and reports were coming in later and later, it made the decision to make a manager change. Within the first two months of hiring a wonderful manager to take charge of the facility, 3MD Storage was on the path to new heights. It realized its manager was the most important asset it had. Having the right manager is priceless.

SMALL CHANGES CAN MAKE A BIG DIFFERENCE

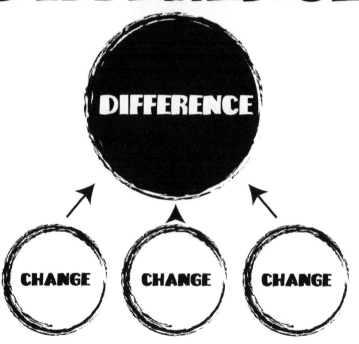

Small Changes Can Make A Big Difference

You have completed many actions that will have a huge impact on the ability of your self storage business to dominate its local market. Congratulations! But you're not done. I hate to break it to you, but you'll never be done. If you want to maintain the improvements you've made, you have to keep doing the things that brought you that success in the first place. Don't get lulled into a false security and allow yourself to slack off. You must work as if the competitor down the street is working every day to take it all away from you. Give up on the idea that you'll someday "arrive." You'll never arrive. Instead of focusing on the results of your efforts to improve your business, focus on the process.

Lack of consistency is a massive vulnerability in this highly competitive industry. It's time to embrace the philosophy of small, continuous improvement. Each day, just focus on getting 1 percent better on a specific aspect of your storage business. That's it. Just 1 percent.

It might not seem like much, but those 1 percent improvements will start compounding on each other. Gradually you'll start to notice the improvements that will come if you just focus on consistently upping your game by 1 percent every day.

Ask yourself this question every single day: What's one small thing I can change that would improve my business? Then start small—like really small. For example, ask yourself:

- How can I phrase my approach better during the rental process to increase autopays?
- How can I get one Google review today?
- How can I take better pictures of my facility for our website?
- How can I make my office smell better to make a better first impression?
- How can my rent-raise letters be more effectively worded?

You get the idea. Think of the smallest step you can take that would move you toward improving your business. Then try to make it even smaller. Take it slow and steady—constant and never-ending improvement!

Once a day, pick up a specific aspect of your storage business (operations, marketing, sales, revenue management, and so on) and analyze how you can make a small improvement. Just a 1 percent improvement.

3miledominators.com
Item: 1% Improvement

Section Six:
3 Mile Domination

Inner Circle

Phew!

Right now you're probably feeling a bit overwhelmed. You've just concluded a full-on immersion course in high-level self storage domination, and you should feel proud of yourself. This book provides you with action steps. Don't read it once and go on with business as usual. Keep it handy, and refer to it often. As I mentioned before, this is about your storage business constantly improving. Day by day. Week by week. Month by month. Year by year.

Many people who read this book before it went to print wanted me to help them with their businesses personally, including sites that were under construction or their existing facilities. I did that for some and was able to identify the holes that were keeping them from growing as fast as they wanted. I suggested the simple tweaks needed to implement these action steps you've just learned about.

That's what I love so much about the things you've learned in this book. They are all simple concepts that you can apply without too much effort, but the results from each of these tweaks can have a profound impact on your storage business.

Once this book is available, I know it's going to be much harder to accommodate everyone who wants more personalized help. So I created something special just for the readers of this book. I've opened up space in our 3 Mile Domination Inner Circle program so that I can personally look at your self storage business, have one-on-one calls each month, and access all the systems to implement the changes you need to make.

If you'd be interested in being a part of our inner circle, then I want to invite you to apply to me personally.

You can apply here:

3miledomination.com/innercircle

After you apply, we will give you a call and explain the Inner Circle program to see if it's a good fit.

Thank you for reading this book, and I wish you all the success in becoming a self storage dominator!

Jim Ross

RESOURCES

83005404R00083

Made in the USA
Columbia, SC
07 December 2017